LINK TO HOPE

One Woman's Journey To Find Her Way

LORIE LINK

Printed in the United States of America

Permissions gratefully acknowledged for quotes from the following copyrighted material:

ISBN-13: 978-1-952208-01-0

Editor's note:
The names, details, and circumstances may have been changed to protect the privacy of those mentioned in this book. This book is for information purposes only. It is not to serve as a substitute for professional medical advice. The publisher and the author disclaim liability for any medical outcomes that may occur as a result of applying the suggestions in this book.

Edited by Kristen Forbes (DeviancePress.com)

Designed by Joni McPherson (McPhersonGraphics.com)

TABLE OF CONTENTS

INTRODUCTION

A few years ago, while sitting in a small bible group study I still regularly attend, a good friend of mine was struggling with losing his job. After listening to his share, I made the well-meaning comment, "I know exactly how you feel."

He looked at me, quite upset, and snapped, "How could you possibly understand what I'm going through!"

I was taken back by that comment and felt rather hurt, until I realized this man had only known me for two years. To him, I had always been happy-and-joyous Lorie. He hadn't witnessed my years of struggle, had never seen me on those days when it took all I had just to get out of bed in the morning. He saw my life as being too perfect for me to relate to his problems. I wanted to make sure that never happened again. I decided to share my story—with all its details—to show people that it's OK to share our problems. **Instead of living behind the veil of perfection, it's OK to not be perfect.** Reach out and get the help you need, wherever you can find it. I can assure you, the people you reach out to are also living with their own imperfections. As women, we need to be available to lift each other up instead of judging one another for our imperfections.

When people meet me today, they may assume by my sunny disposition that nothing tragic has ever happened to me, that I've never experienced real struggle. It's common in our society to believe that if someone has been through a tragedy, they simply can't recover; they are doomed to always be a shadow of their former selves, a lost soul.

But I assure you this isn't the case! I have lived through the deaths of loved ones, through divorce, job losses, and poverty, and yet I made it through to the other side. And if I can do it? Trust me, you can definitely do it.

Over the years, I've discovered two main reasons some people never heal from their trauma. The first is the desire to be perfect. For years, I suffered through my problems alone, determined to maintain an outward appearance of perfection to my friends and family. Rather than be open and honest about whatever was falling apart in my world, I just put on a smile. I didn't want to burden others with my problems. I didn't realize that by doing this, I was making all my problems that much worse.

To illustrate my point, think about the last time you started dating someone who had a mannerism you really disliked. Maybe they chewed gum with their mouth open or never put the cap back on the toothpaste. Whatever it was, you likely ignored it for weeks, maybe even months; you'd see that toothpaste oozing out of the tube, take a deep breath, and just go on about your day. But slowly you built up resentment about this little action until one day—when you were in a particularly foul mood after work—you yelled at your partner for this minor transgression. Your partner, completely unaware that this was bothering you, felt blind sighted and hurt. In the end, you have made the situation much worse than it needed to be.

Now think about how you could have better handled the situation. You could have saved yourself a lot of time by simply mentioning the bad habit early on in a nice way. "Hey good-looking, would you mind putting the cap back on that? It's a silly pet peeve of mine." It would've been no big deal. But since you waited and let that pressure build and then explode, you ended up looking like a cruel, overbearing partner who gets mad about *toothpaste.* All problems work this same way; the longer you keep them to yourself, the more they intensify, and the more power you give them. Instead of bottling everything up, release things as they come. That way, you never get to the blow-up stage.

▶ LESSON 1

Perfection is a myth.

The first thing I want you to learn from this book is that **perfection is a myth**. Let go of your need to seem perfect to those around you. Why? People who chase perfection tend not to reach out for help. They don't want to appear weak or have others think less of them. In the perfectionist's mind, if she asks for help, others will judge her and think less of her. Unfortunately, due in part to social media, we seem to live in a perfect society. We only want others to see our "best selves." We take multiple selfies before we find the perfect one with the perfect angle. We only post the happiest pictures of our family, the extravagant vacations, the beautiful food we eat.

But perfection is a myth. Don't be afraid to reach out and show your imperfect self. It doesn't make you less of a person. Your true friends will be there for you no matter how "imperfect" you are—in fact, they will probably be relieved to know you're just like them! The more you show your true self to others, and the more vulnerable you are with them, the more they will trust you with their own vulnerabilities. By opening up and showing your true self, you can find support and strengthen your bonds with those around you. So, it's okay not to be perfect. No one is!

By picking up this book, you've already taken the first step. You have admitted to yourself that you can't do this alone, that you need something other than yourself to get you through whatever you may be dealing with. However, you must continue to fight against that need for perfection. You must be willing to rely on more than yourself and this book, and to eventually reach out to those in the world around you—whether it's your partner, a family member, or a licensed professional.

▶ LESSON 2

You're addicted to your pain.

The second reason many people don't recover from trauma is because they become addicted to the pain. *Addicted to the pain? But that's ludicrous,* you're thinking. After all, pain is painful, so why would we want to prolong it? But consider this for a second. Have you ever stayed in bed too long, becoming increasingly anxious about your day, knowing you'd feel better if you just got up, but decided to stay in bed anyway? Or think about your last breakup—whether it was last night or last millennium—did you sulk in those bad feelings? Did you spend just a few too many nights crying over a carton of Ben & Jerry's simply because it felt easier than getting dressed and going for a walk?

Most of the time, we intuitively know what's best for us. Our conscience—that little voice in our head—tells us we'll feel better after we take a shower, clean the house, take a walk, or get some work done. But the human in you, the one addicted to pain and self-pity, prefers to wallow. So, I ask you, are you done wallowing? Are you ready to fully listen to your conscience, to do what you know you need to do in order to heal? By becoming aware of your addiction to pain, you've already gained power over it. The next time you're ready to crawl under the covers and over-analyze your life, listen to your conscience instead. Pick up this book, get out of the house, or call a friend. **You have much more power over your pain than you think.**

That being said, sometimes our grief is so overwhelming that we can't function, make decisions, or physically get out of bed. I've been there. That's when you need to make the choice to get help, because you can't do this alone.

In this book, we'll discuss grief and loss. Though I've suffered through many hardships in my life, I've always found my way back. Your grief can lead you on a journey that you never expected, which is exactly what happened to me. I'm an ordinary woman with an extraordinary story to share. And if in that story others can see themselves and realize that no matter what, there is hope for the future and a way to have a happier life, then I have fulfilled my purpose.

I'll offer you the tools to persevere through difficult circumstances and various forms of loss, whether it's the loss of a job, friends, romantic love, a parent, or even a child. I'll show you how to live life on life's terms and how to view life's obstacles as opportunities for growth. And, perhaps most importantly, I'll help you find or increase your spiritual connection with a higher power.

Embrace this journey. Embrace your freedom to be imperfect. Forgive yourself for being human, for needing help. Surrender to this experience and open your heart and mind to the possibility of healing. **You *can* heal. You *deserve* to heal.**

CHAPTER 1

My story starts when I was a junior in high school. I was the typical outgoing, popular girl on the cheerleading squad, and my peers voted me Miss CHS. I was *very* sure of myself.

I was raised in a loving but strict and conservative southern Christian home. I was the youngest of four girls, the baby of the family. Our parents were amazing, but we were extremely sheltered from the outside world. At the time, we didn't realize we were sheltered; that's just the way things were. Our lives consisted of home, family, church, and school.

My mother was the disciplinarian of the family, while my dad was the pushover. If we wanted something, we would soften Daddy up first, then let him work on Mom. When we got into trouble, Dad's favorite saying was, "Honey, don't do that cause I'm going to have to get your Mama, and you know what she's going to do to you!"

He was the sweetest, kindest man I have ever known. He had the ability to make you feel like you were the most important person in the entire world.

For as long as I can remember, our mother had two wishes: we would grow up and live for God, and we would marry good Christian men. Sounds easy, right? I thought, you grow up, find a good man (just like my father), marry him, and live happily ever after. At least, that's what everyone in my family had always done.

Every Sunday, we attended a small country church. If thirty people were in attendance, that was a huge crowd. Our father led the singing, and our mother always made sure the preacher had food after church. We didn't have a full-time preacher. Typically, bible students from Freed Hardeman College (a local Christian College) would come and "practice preaching" with us.

I enjoyed church. During my teenage years, there were times I didn't really want to go, but I always did. It wasn't an option not to go. Going to church wasn't just somewhere we went on Sunday; it was a way of life in our home. It was a simple life, but we liked it that way.

When I was a junior in high school, we built a new house and moved closer to town. My brother-in-law Brad was the music minister at the big church in town, and I decided to go there on Sunday evenings. My sister Gail told me they had a youth group. *Hmmm,* that was a new concept. We didn't have a youth group at our regular church. We had very few youths, so therefore no group.

The first night I went to the youth group meeting, I saw several kids I knew from school. I'd had no idea they attended this church. As I looked around the room, I saw someone I had seen at school but didn't really know, Tim. He was the quiet kid in school that always wore black-rimmed glasses and stayed in the background. But when we first met at church, he had shed his usual glasses for contacts, which almost made it hard to recognize him. I was drawn to him immediately—he was gorgeous! I thought, *Wow . . . I didn't know he went to church . . . He's hot and he's a Christian! I think my mother would definitely approve.*

We started dating junior year. Living in a small town, dating usually consisted of going out to the Tastee Freeze and a movie. He would sit by me in church, and we'd call and talk on the phone for hours. I was a cheerleader so he would offer to drive me home after the games. Ironically, when his parents decided to build a new house, guess where they bought the land? Right next door to our house. He literally became the boy next door.

Before we knew it, we were inseparable. We were voted cutest couple and were having the time of our lives. We did everything together, told each other our secrets, and were crazy in love. Of course, we were only seventeen years old, so we were as in love as two teenagers could be. At that time, love to me was a feeling, it was the attention he gave me and the friendship we shared. My days were consumed with getting to spend time with him. I could not imagine my life without Tim.

We dated throughout the rest of high school and graduated in June. I had always been a good student, so my parents had assumed I would go on to college, as two of my sisters had both gone to a Christian college. All through high school, I had assumed I would go to college, but I hadn't ever thought about what I wanted to study or what career path I would choose. I thought that once I started and got the basics out of the way, I would at some point choose a career that interested me. At that time, I hadn't been exposed to women who had careers. They had jobs, but not necessarily careers. My sister Karen was a huge influence on my life. She attended college and worked for a judge immediately after graduating. But after my high school graduation, I decided not to go to college, and instead got a job at the county courthouse in the County Court Clerk's office.

At some point after high school, Tim started hanging out with different people, partying and drinking, which was out of character for him. But during high school, we all partied from time to time, so I truly believed he was just going through a phase. My mother sat me down because she had heard things about him, and of course I defended him. She wanted me to break up with him, but being a teenager, the more she bashed Tim, the more I wanted to be with him.

Tim remained my priority. And just like every teenager who falls in love, the prospect of sex started consuming my thoughts and our conversations. Being religious, I saw sex as a moral dilemma. But I was young and in love, and I thought I had my whole life ahead of me. I wanted to make my own decisions and be an adult. I'd always been the baby of the family, and I didn't want to be that anymore. I tried to justify my actions by thinking we were going to get married anyway—so what was the harm?

Then, one morning, I woke up feeling sick and throwing up. The next day, the same thing happened. When it happened again on the third day, I suspected I may be pregnant. I was so scared. I couldn't tell my parents, so I prayed to God to please not let me be pregnant. At this point, I started bargaining with God. I prayed, "God, if you will let me not be pregnant, I will never do anything bad again ever in my life." Well, as you might guess, that didn't go so well.

I lay awake at night trying to figure out how I was going to tell my parents. One morning, my mother came into my room, lay down on the bed with me, and said, "I want to ask you a question. Are you pregnant?"

I couldn't believe my ears. Evidently, she had heard me throwing up the past few mornings and had put two and two together. She lay on the bed and cried, and I cried with her. "I'm sorry, I'm sorry," I said.

I could see the disappointment in her face. She said, "Please let *me* tell your father, because this news will devastate him." I loved my father more than life itself, and I couldn't bear seeing the disappointment in his face. I prayed to God that this was a mistake and I wasn't really pregnant.

The next day, my parents called me into the living room and told me my dad was going to take me to the doctor to confirm the pregnancy.

I cried while my dad comforted me. He gently put his arm around me and all he said was, "It's going to be alright. We love you and will be here no matter what."

Wow, that hadn't been the reaction I was expecting, but I think my mother had broken the news to him and he, in his loving and understanding way, was trying to make it okay for me. That was how my father always made me feel, like everything was going to be okay. But if the truth be known, I think we were all praying it was all a mistake and I just had the flu.

But we went to the doctor and it was confirmed: I was pregnant. I was eighteen, unmarried, and pregnant. How could I have let this happen? I knew right from wrong, and my parents had raised me right. How was I ever going to live through all the embarrassment and shame? Because in my world, it was shameful for my family.

At that time, typically the right thing to do in this situation was to get married as soon as possible so no one would know the baby had been conceived prior to marriage. I thought this was what my parents would insist upon, so when they asked me if Tim knew, I said no, that I had wanted to make sure I was actually pregnant before saying anything.

My parents insisted the next step was to tell Tim and his parents, but my mother added, "Whatever you do, don't think you are going to marry him. You are eighteen years old, and marriage is forever." I listened, but in the back of my mind I thought, *This is what I have always wanted, to be married to my Christian husband and have a family*. In my eighteen-year-old brain, I was just doing things backwards.

I called Tim and told him we needed to talk. We went out that evening and I told him the news. He was shocked but immediately said that he loved me, and that we should get married. After all, this was what we had always planned; we were just moving a little faster than we'd expected. He wanted time to tell his parents, and after a few days, we decided we were going to get married.

My parents were not happy. We had always been taught that you should take your time finding your spouse because marriage is forever. No one in my family had ever gotten divorced. At that time, I don't think I even *knew* anyone who had been divorced. They begged me not to get married. They even said they would help me raise the baby. But in our eighteen-year-old brains, we thought we were doing the right thing.

On April 20th, we were married at my parents' home with only family and our closest friends in attendance. We didn't buy traditional wedding clothes; I wore a blue flower dress and Tim, a blue suit. We each had a friend stand up with us as maid of honor and best man. There was cake and punch afterwards. Most girls dream of a big wedding, but I had never pictured that. My sister Gail had a big wedding, and while I thought it was beautiful, a big wedding wasn't something I had hoped for. So, for Tim and me, it was a happy, joyous occasion. We were young and in love and starting our family. But all our parents could see was the mistake we were making. Still, they were as supportive as they could be.

I often get asked what it was like to be a pregnant teenager. It's funny, because I didn't think of myself as a pregnant teen, even though I obviously was! In my brain, I was an adult, making adult decisions and doing adult things. It was hard though, watching all my friends go off to college, doing college things. My life was so different from theirs. When they would come home and tell me about the things they were doing, there was a part of me that wanted that part of my life back.

In the beginning of the pregnancy I was in denial, like at some point I was going to wake up and it would have all been a dream. The idea of being a mother didn't sink in for quite some time. I had an amazing mother as a role model, so my idea of being a mother was the way I had been raised. I read books, talked to women who had babies, and tried to get as much information on taking care of a baby as I possibly could. But as I soon realized, nothing could have prepared me for what I was about to experience.

My pregnancy was difficult. The first six months, I threw up twice a day, every day. It was exhausting. The doctors gave me medication to help with the sickness, but nothing helped, so I was able to wear my normal clothes until I was almost seven months pregnant. I had also started a new job right after the wedding and being that sick every day was really draining.

But even with all the things that should've been wrong—being so young and pregnant, trying to work and being so sick—I was happy in my life with Tim. We had a little life and family that I loved. Obviously, there were people who looked at us and judged our life, but I tried not to let that bother me.

Life doesn't always go as planned—in fact, it hardly ever goes as planned! Although the timing of my pregnancy wasn't at all what I had pictured for myself, it happened, and I learned to make the best of it. Whatever you may be dealing with right now, it won't get any better if you fight it. You must learn to live life on life's terms, which we'll continue to work on throughout this book. For now, let's start with a simple prayer you can say whenever you're feeling a loss of control over your life, the serenity prayer:

> *"God, grant me the serenity to*
> *accept the things I cannot change,*
>
> *The courage to change the things I*
> *can,*
>
> *And the wisdom to know the*
> *difference."*

✻ EXERCISE 1

Expanding the Serenity Prayer

Expand upon the serenity prayer by adding in the things you cannot change, as well as the things you can. This exercise will help you process your feelings about whatever transition you're going through, as well as help you stay focused on what you *can* change.

I'll illustrate with an example. Let's say you recently lost your job as a receptionist. Here is what the expanded serenity prayer may look like:

"God, grant me the serenity to accept the things I cannot change.

I **cannot** *change the fact that I've lost my job. My boss is retiring, and her replacement is bringing her own receptionist with her. I'm no longer needed for the position. I accept this.*

God, grant me the courage to change the things I can.

I **can** *change the way I react to the layoff. I'm going to send my boss a nice card to tell her how much I've appreciated the past four years working for her. I'm going to finish out my last week at the office on a strong, graceful note I can be proud of.*

I **can** *change my attitude about the layoff. I choose to see this as an opportunity to finally go back to school for nursing. This was just the push I needed. I had gotten too comfortable there. I had originally planned* *to only be a receptionist for a year, and I just never had the courage to leave!*

God, grant me the wisdom to know the difference. I will continue to realize that what's done is done; I ***cannot*** *get my old job back, but I* ***can*** *change how I handle this transition."*

Try reciting this expanded prayer every time life throws you a curveball. Instead of focusing on what you *can't* change, you'll feel empowered by what you *can*.

CHAPTER 2

One month shy of my nineteenth birthday, on November 16th, David was born. When I first came home from the hospital, Tim was working the midnight shift at a correctional facility as a prison guard. I didn't want to be by myself, so I stayed at my parents' house for a week to enlist their help. The first two days and nights, David cried almost without stopping. It was on day three that Tim and I looked at each other and said, "Oh my god, what have we done?" We realized we had no idea what it meant to be parents or how to care for a child. But day by day, with our parents' help, we learned to get through the days.

When I look back at those first few months, it's funny what I remember. I still recall the way David looked at me when they first put him into my arms. He was so tiny and helpless, but he had these gigantic blue eyes that looked right at me, as though he knew exactly who I was. At that moment, I realized that it was no longer about me; I was now responsible for another human being, and everything changed.

When David was a baby, my relationship with him was all about taking care of his basic needs, making sure he had everything he needed to survive. When he was a baby, I loved dressing him in cute outfits, almost as I had done with my dolls when I was a little girl (actually, I still was a little girl!). Bonding with David was easy; I felt bonded to him the minute I saw him. Birthdays and Christmas, even ordinary days, took on a whole new meaning by seeing everything through his eyes.

My parents adored David. He stayed with them while I worked during the day at the courthouse. My mother became my biggest helper, teaching me how to do the most basic "mother things." My father would hold David, lift him up to his face, look right into his eyes, and just talk very softly to him. He would rock and sing him to sleep every day. My father would make his usual trip into town with David and stop by the courthouse to say hello and that he loved me.

Then one day, after one of my Dad's morning visits, I got a call from my mother to come home. My father had suffered a massive coronary. By the time we got to the hospital, he was gone. I was beyond devastated. I had just seen him at 10 o'clock that morning, and he'd been fine. I couldn't believe God would cause this to happen. My father had been my rock, and I couldn't believe God would take him away at this point in my life. I needed him. I needed his strength. No matter what had ever been going on in my life, my father had always been able to make everything okay.

For weeks, I attempted to work. I found myself going through the motions of life, but mostly I cried—a lot. Having a four-month-old child kept me busy, but I spent a lot of time wondering if I had missed an important sign that day when my father visited me. Was there something I could have done to recognize that something was wrong? After all, I had just seen him four hours before he'd had the heart attack. But in the end, there was nothing. He had been his normal loving self that day. There was a sadness inside me I had never experienced before. It affected my personality, my mood, everything about me. I purposely didn't visit his grave; it was too painful for me. Maybe if I didn't see it, it wasn't real?

My mother was heartbroken. She had married my father when she was only fifteen years old, and he was the love of her life. She was so lost. We tried to help her, but she was beyond devastated. When I think of my mother, there was the mother before my father died, and the mother after. She became very withdrawn and almost bitter. She no longer found enjoyment in anything. She cried at the drop of a hat, lost her temper easily, and began to rely on pills that the doctor had given her to help her get through the funeral service. Once we realized this, we very quickly took those away from her. At first, she wasn't happy with that decision, but she later thanked us for looking out for her when she couldn't make decisions on her own. This was our first experience with grief, and none of us really knew what to do except to be sad and try to get through each day.

My siblings and I always believed my mother never got over the loss of my father. She never remarried or even dated, that we knew of, though she was still a young woman when my father died, only forty-nine. She went on with life, but there was always a sadness within her, and the joyous woman we knew was gone. She was a woman of faith and relied on that to get her through the days. She was also a servant to others. Her greatest joy, other than her family, was cooking for people and inviting them into her home. She would have happy moments and went on to have a full life, but the sadness was ever present. All her life, she wrote poetry. Some she shared with us, but most of her writings were not discovered until after her death. We found several notebooks full of her poetry, many about how she felt about our dad and the grief and sadness within her. It was very eye-opening to me and my sisters to read her inner thoughts.

Mom had an extremely close relationship with David; she had always kept him while I worked, but she was in such a bad place that I made the decision to get someone else to watch him, at least for a while, until she could get control of her life again. She insisted that she be the one to keep him; it gave her some sense of purpose to be with him and take care of him. But at this time, he was still a baby, so the relationship was a little one-sided. As the years went by, they became extremely close.

I prayed that God would help us through this difficult time. In my head, I knew that my father was a Christian, and would be with God, but my selfishness wanted him here with me. That was the first experience I'd ever had with grieving. As time went on, I came to realize that death was a part of life. I wasn't happy about it, didn't totally understand or agree with it, but it was one of those lessons in life that you had to accept, learn from, and move on from. Of course, I would have loved to have had my father here for much longer. He was only sixty years old when he died. But my father and the lessons he taught me, and his influence, have never left me. I am the person I am today because of how I was brought up by my parents.

Sometimes simply understanding what you're going through can help. Let's discuss the stages of grief and how they may present themselves to you. None of these stages are wrong or should be avoided; they are all natural responses to grief, and you should not rush through any of them. You do not have to go through each stage in order to heal. You may also not experience them in sequential order.

1. **Denial & Isolation: "This can't be happening."**

   Denying what has happened is a normal reaction, especially to an unexpected or sudden death. Denial buffers the immediate shock of the loss, numbing us to our emotions [REF https://psychcentral.com/lib/the-5-stages-of-loss-and-grief/]. This is a temporary response that carries us through the first wave of pain. This stage is nature's way of only letting in as much as we can handle. As you begin to accept reality, you will start the healing process. As denial fades and you become stronger, all the feelings you were denying will begin to surface in the later stages.

3. **Anger: "Why did this happen? Who is to blame?"**

   Your anger after the death of a loved "one" could be directed at any number of targets. When my father passed, I directed my anger toward God. You may even target your anger at your deceased loved one, due to resentment towards them for causing you this pain. Another convenient target may be the doctor or health professional who was unable to cure your loved one's disease. Don't hesitate to ask your doctor to explain again the details of your loved one's illness. Getting clear answers to your questions can help you find closure.

4. **Bargaining: "Make this not happen and I will..."**

When my father passed and I kept looking back on his courthouse visit to look for signs, I was in the bargaining stage of my grief. Some common thoughts during this phase are "If only we'd gone to the doctor sooner," or "If only I'd answered their phone call."

A lot of guilt usually accompanies this phase. What could we have done differently to have avoided this death? Many people find themselves stuck in this stage for prolonged periods of time, which can lead to depression. Be sure to reach out for professional help if you find yourself feeling the associated symptoms.

4. **Depression: "I can't bear this. I'm too sad to do anything."**

   In this stage, you might withdraw and isolate yourself. You may feel numb, in a fog, or not want to get out of bed. You may experience feelings of hopelessness or even suicidal thoughts. After losing a loved one, it can be difficult to find value in life or think, "What's the point?"

5. **Acceptance: "I acknowledge what has happened, and I cannot change it."**

   This stage is often confused with "being okay" with what has happened, but that's not the case. This stage is just about accepting your new reality, that your loved one is physically gone and is not coming back. You learn to live with the loss. You readjust to your new life and begin to live again.

   When you begin to enjoy life again, you may feel like you're betraying your loved one. But don't deny yourself the rest of your life.

Now that you know a bit about what to expect during the various phrases of grief, let's talk about healthy ways to cope with the pain:

1. **Don't expect to be ready for the natural order of things; you won't be.**

   As I mentioned, I couldn't work for weeks. Experts recommend taking time off from work if you can, though of course not everyone is able to go without pay for weeks at a time, and not all workplaces grant paid bereavement leave.

When you do go back to work—whenever that may be—you will likely still find it difficult to jump right back into your daily workload. Don't be hard on yourself if you aren't performing to your usual standard or can't focus for long periods of time. Take lots of breaks or step outside for a breath of fresh air when you're feeling overwhelmed with your grief. And if you're able to, plan a slow return to work, possibly even starting out part-time or working from home.

All, getting back into a routine can help some people with their grief.

2. **You are entitled to grieve in whichever way feels right to you.**

Don't let family members, friends, or coworkers make you feel badly about however you may be expressing your grief. Do not feel hurried to get through the grieving process. It is an extremely personal process that is unique to each individual and each loss.

3. **Express your feelings in a tangible or creative way.**

   Write down your feelings in a journal. Research shows that writing about stressful events can help you come to terms with them, acting as a stress management tool. Journaling can also help you track your progress and find any patterns that may arise in your grief.

4. **Be kind to yourself.**

   The bereavement period is associated with elevated risk for the onset of multiple psychiatric disorders, including depression, anxiety, and substance abuse [REF: https://www.ncbi.nlm.nih.gov/pmc/articles/PMC4119479/]. It's important to take care of yourself during this time to reduce your risk of developing these disorders. Book a babysitter if you need a night to yourself without the kids or treat yourself to your favorite spa package. Reducing your stress levels early on will help prevent serious health consequences.

5. **Seek support.**

   Reach out and talk about it with someone you trust, whether it's a friend, family member, or licensed professional. A psychologist can help you build your resilience and develop strategies for getting through your sadness.

   Support groups can also be a beneficial way to get through the worst of your grieving. Sharing your sorrow with others who have experienced a similar loss can really help you feel less alone in your grief.

6. **Preserve your memories.**

   Create a tribute to your loved one by planting a tree or garden, or by taking part in a charity run or walk. Make a memory box that has reminders of the person who died and include photos or whatever else you choose. When you're missing the person, write them a letter and "send" it to them by putting it in the box.

7. **Rely on your faith.**

   Rely on your faith to get you through the tough days. Whatever spiritual activities are meaningful to you—whether praying, meditating, or going to church—keep doing them. If you're questioning your faith due to a loss, talk to a member or leader of your religious community to find some perspective. Know it is natural to question faith during the grieving process, but that it does not mean you have lost your connection forever.

Grieving is a process, and it's okay to be sad. It's okay to cry. Remember that the memories you've made with your loved one will live on forever. Though I wish I'd had more time with my dad, and that he was still here to share special moments with me today, he will always live on in my heart.

CHAPTER 3

By our third wedding anniversary, my marriage to Tim was already in serious trouble. Surprise, right? Some nights he chose not to come home at all. Whenever he *was* home, it was just one big argument. Being so young, neither one of us understood the responsibility of marriage, and it was taking its toll. There were many nights when after an argument, he would stay out all night and not come home. I was trying to be a good mother and put on a happy face for our parents, since divorce wasn't an option.

That year, David and I went to my mother's home for Thanksgiving dinner. I felt like I couldn't share any of my problems with her because she was still grieving for my dad. She was still dealing with her own problems, so how would she able to help me with mine? So, I kept my marriage problems to myself, and again, I put on a happy front.

Tim never came to family dinners, so it wasn't unusual that he wasn't there with us. I told my mom that he had to work, which of course was a total lie That evening, when David and I got home, Tim wasn't there. But since he was never home, I didn't think it was that unusual. Then, there was a knock at the door. When I answered it, standing in front of me was one of Tim's friends.

He said, "Lorie, I don't know how to tell you this"—any time a sentence starts with those words, you know it's not going to end well—"but Tim is in jail."

I was stunned. "Why, what did he do?" I asked.

He told me that Tim had been a passenger in a car that was pulled over by the police and searched. During the search, there was an altercation between Tim and the officer, which resulted in the officer being taken to the hospital.

Tim was charged with a Class X felony and was facing ten years in prison if found guilty.

I completely broke down. Never in my wildest dreams could I have imagined this was how my Thanksgiving would end. I had no idea what to do. My father was dead, my mother was grieving, I was twenty-one years old with a baby, and now my husband was facing ten years in prison. I sat in a chair and cried uncontrollably for what seemed like hours. I had no idea what to do, so I turned to God and said, "Please help me. God, why am I having to go through this? I don't understand."

Finally, I put my son in the car, drove to my sister Judy's house, and literally fell in the door when she opened it. After a few minutes, I was finally able to tell her what had happened, not just about Tim's arrest but also about our marital problems. I hadn't wanted anyone to know just how hard things had gotten, and I had previously kept my problems to myself. Looking back, I feared being judged or looked down upon by others. I didn't want people to think I was too weak to handle situations. There were plenty of people that were waiting to say "I told you so" or that we were too young to get married, so I chose to handle my issues the best way I knew how. But dealing—or, not dealing—with problems this way can do a great deal of harm.

Instead, get help and reach out to someone you trust. Any time you talk about your problems out loud to another person, it somehow takes the problem's power away and makes it less scary. Sometimes you don't even need the other person to respond, you just need to get it off your chest. Sharing problems with someone is always easier. A load is often lighter when there is someone to help you carry it. Sometimes we need an answer that is not so obvious to us alone. Sharing with someone you trust, or a professional, may help guide you in a direction you never knew was available. Another person can provide a different perspective on your problem, or help you see its solution more clearly.

After talking to my sister, I called and broke the news to Tim's family, but I still couldn't call my own mother. I didn't believe she could handle it. Judy decided she would go over to our mother's house the next day and break the news to her in person.

In a small town, news like this spreads like wildfire. The local newspapers, TV stations, and radio stations were discussing the attack on a local police officer. The following Monday, I was fired from my job. My boss said that he was cutting back and didn't need me anymore. That evening, I picked up David at the babysitter's, and she pulled me aside to talk. She said she had been struggling with so many children and needed to cut back. She asked if I could find someone else to watch David. Even people I had known all my life would turn their heads when they saw me walk towards them. It was a terrible, isolating feeling.

We borrowed the money to hire a lawyer and went through a three-week trial process. In the end, Tim was sentenced to three years in the state prison, but only served approximately half of the sentence due to good behavior.

When Tim went to prison, my mother told me I had to divorce him. I couldn't believe those words were coming out of her mouth. The word *divorce* wasn't spoken in our home. It felt really good to have her support, though. It was validation that she really understood what I was going through. It's easy to say something is "wrong" until it hits home and affects your family, then you begin to see things in a totally different way. I saw this in my mother.

After everything I had been through, I knew I couldn't put my son through this anymore. Once I made the decision, I met with a lawyer to discuss the case. According to the law, if I divorced my husband while he was in prison, I wasn't entitled to any child support. I didn't think I could raise David without financial help, so I decided to wait it out and serve the papers as soon as Tim was out of prison.

While he was in prison, Tim began writing to me. He told me he was meeting regularly with the chaplain and was turning his life around. He said he'd learned his lesson and would do anything to get his family back. I really wanted to believe that.

After two years, he was released from prison for good behavior. In the beginning, he seemed so different. I decided to give him another chance. He had changed, and he was back to being the person I had fallen in love with . . . for a little while.

Then little by little, we started arguing again. It was non-stop, and the relationship went downhill very quickly. One day, the argument became so volatile that I could no longer stay in the relationship, nor could I allow my son to live in this environment. I abruptly left with only my son. I again showed up on my mother's doorstep needing a place to live.

I explained to her what had happened, and as usual, she took us in without question. Once I settled into my mother's home, I came to the stark reality that I had left with no money, no clothes, and at that time, no job.

Eventually, day by day, I was able to get back on my feet. I made the decision to divorce Tim. I knew I had to; I couldn't keep putting my son through the chaos. He didn't deserve to live like that. Like everything else, the divorce wasn't easy. But finally, after six years of marriage, our divorce was final.

The divorce was another loss of someone I'd once loved. I had to go through a different form of grief. When I lost my father, I grieved for the love and devotion I'd had for him. I grieved that we wouldn't be able to make any new memories, and that I would no longer see him and share that love. With the divorce, I grieved the loss and devotion that could have been but wasn't. I grieved the memories that couldn't be made because we could no longer find the love that had initially brought us together. Even with all the chaos of our married life, the day the divorce was final, I cried. I mourned for what could have been. I mourned that I had failed at marriage. I mourned a relationship that had begun with so much love. The finality of divorce and the failure made my cry.

That being said, in many ways the divorce was a relief. I was just happy to get me and my son out of the chaos and get on with my life. David didn't deserve to live the life we'd been living. My driving force was to make a better life for my son.

While I don't take marriage lightly, it was the only choice I had under the circumstances. If you're currently questioning a romantic relationship in your life, you must do what is right for you and your family. Consider all your options carefully.

In the previous chapter, we discussed the five stages of grief as they apply to the death of a loved one. Many professionals also apply these same five stages to the experience of divorce. Whether you're on the receiving end or the initiating end of the divorce, you will likely spend at least some time in all five stages. Just like with grieving a death, do not rush through any of the stages, and don't be concerned if you don't experience them in sequential order or exactly as described. Move through each phase at your own pace and be easy on yourself as you heal.

1. **Denial: "I can't believe it's over."**

   If you didn't initiate the divorce, you may spend a significant amount of time in the denial stage. This stage can even lead to a delay in finalizing the divorce. When I married Tim, I had fully expected us to stay together forever; divorce was the furthest thing from my mind. You likely felt similarly when marrying your former partner. It can be challenging to wrap your head around divorce, especially if you've been married for a long period of time or have children with your former partner.

You might even talk yourself into thinking that the breakup is only temporary. You may not truly let yourself believe things are over; this is your mind trying to protect you from feeling overwhelmed. Try getting used to the idea that the relationship is over for now, and likely forever. Try to get past the fantasy of getting back together.

Allow yourself time to process your new reality. It will seem overwhelming at first, whether you initiated the divorce or not. It *is* a big change, and you're validated in feeling whatever emotions you're experiencing.

2. **Anger: "He ruined my life!"**

   Divorce can be drenched in blame and rage. You may find yourself frequently dissecting all the events in your marriage, rehashing every argument and wrong done to you by your ex-partner. It is okay to *feel* anger, *write* about your anger, and *talk* about your anger, but be careful not to act out due to your anger—this can have consequences! When you're in this stage, be fully aware of your animosity and its influence over you. Acknowledge it and deal with it in healthy ways, whether it's signing up for a kickboxing class or talking to a therapist.

If you don't deal with your anger in healthy ways, you may make hostile and vindictive decisions that could come back to haunt you. Remember to do what's best for your family. Take care of yourself so that the stress of the situation doesn't consume you and lead you to commit irrational acts.

Be aware: your partner will also go through this phase. If they end up saying or doing anything hurtful, know it is because of their own emotions and issues. Try not to take it too personally—though I know that's easier said than done!

3. **Bargaining: "I've made a huge mistake."**

   Even if you initiate the divorce, you may still struggle with the bargaining stage. You'll experience it as feelings of doubt and guilt that this is the right decision. As the news of the divorce spreads, you may be displeased with the reactions of your friends, family, and coworkers. Just know that it's common to go back and forth during this stage. Try to remember why you wanted the divorce in the first place. What happened has happened and going back now isn't going to fix the problems that caused you to break up in the first place.

   If you didn't initiate the divorce, you could spend quite a bit of time in this stage. You may find yourself pleading with your former partner to "take you back." Before taking any action, try to see the relationship for what it really was. As you ruminate on your history, the mind can be sneaky and focus on the good times. But think about *all* of your times with that person. It will help you process the breakup, and then eventually let go of your ex-partner.

4. **Depression: "I'm lost without him."**

   When you've broken up with someone, their absence will cause you emotional discomfort. You will likely experience unpredictable moments of intense, searing pain. This is normal, don't be frightened; you are not going crazy. You are simply grieving. The pain won't last forever.

   This can be the longest and most difficult stage. Try to remember that this is the storm before the calm, before you find peace. Find a support system and lean on it hard. Ask for and accept help from others. Seek counseling for yourself and your children if they are also struggling.

   Though pain during a divorce is normal, deep depression and suicidal thoughts are not. Seek professional help immediately if you're feeling any signs of clinical depression.

5. **Acceptance: "I'm over it."**

   Embrace your hope for the future! Though you may still find yourself periodically sad or angry about the divorce, you will begin to find peace. This is a time to reclaim who you were before your marriage and welcome all change coming your way. It's time to build a new, better life!

   After I accepted my divorce and began moving on with my life, I found it rewarding to help others going through similar circumstances. When you do in fact find peace after your loss, try to help others heal. When we let each other know what pain we've experienced, and show that we survived it, we provide each other hope for healing.

CHAPTER 4

After the divorce, I went through a period of time where I kept trying to better myself—and I kept failing. I tried to get into nursing school but failed the exam. I also attempted to get a job with the state of Tennessee, I took a test twice, but again I failed . . . twice.

Hitting Rock Bottom

Sitting on my mom's couch, knowing I had failed three times to get a job, I hit my rock bottom. My self-esteem was at an all-time low. I felt completely worthless and trapped in a life I hadn't planned for and hadn't bargained for. I took a long look at myself. How had I gotten to this point? I'd been a popular, confident girl in high school. I'd had my entire life ahead of me. I'd grown up in a wonderful home with Christian parents who supported me. What had gone wrong? I didn't know where that person had gone or how to get her back. And honestly, I wasn't even sure if I wanted her back—after all, she was the one who had gotten me into this mess!

But there's something beautiful about hitting a rock bottom (and I do believe we don't all just have *one* bottom—but rather each phase of our lives includes at least one!): hitting bottom gives you a solid foundation to build upon! It can catapult you into transformation. Without hitting bottom first, many people wouldn't have the motivation or true desire to make a change. That doesn't mean your bottom needs to be as dramatic or devastating as bankruptcy, jail, etc.—though that's okay if that's the case! What it means is that you need to hit *your* bottom, which is simply the point where you aren't willing to go down any further.

One famous rock bottom is that of JK Rowling, the author of the popular *Harry*

Potter book series. Rowling says, "Rock bottom became the solid foundation on which I rebuilt my life." She even wrote a book, *Very Good Lives: The Fringe Benefits of Failure and the Importance of Imagination,* about hitting bottom and the benefits of failure. Rowling rose from impoverished single mother to world-famous author. She considers failure an important aspect because "it is a stripping away of the inessential. I stopped pretending to myself that I was anything other than what I was and began directing all my energy into finishing the only work that mattered to me. Had I really succeeded at anything else, I may never have found the determination to succeed in the one arena where I truly belonged. I was set free because my greatest fear had been realized and I was still alive and still had a daughter whom I adored. And I had an old typewriter and a big idea."

If you've hit your rock bottom, you're now free to really figure out what you want. Try to view your situation as the beginning of something wonderful.

✻ EXERCISE

What if you kept digging?

If you continue on your current path and keep digging and lowering your bottom, what could happen? What are you willing to do to avoid these consequences?

Around the time of my rock bottom, my sister Gail and her family moved to East Peoria, IL, where my brother-in-law Brad was the minister for the East Peoria Church of Christ. Gail was one of the few people that knew the details of what I was going through, and she asked me to come for a visit to get away from all the chaos. East Peoria was a seven-hour drive away, and at the time I had never driven farther than two hours from home. Money was really tight, but I really wanted to go. She told me that the Amtrak train stopped in Bloomington, IL, and if I would take the train, she would pick me up at the station.

Here's how naïve I was. I drove to Brad's mom's house in Missouri (where the closest train station was located), and she took David and I to the Amtrak station at three in the morning. Now, I had never been on a train in my life. When we boarded, a man directed us to go upstairs and to "be prepared" because there weren't any empty seats. We headed upstairs, and I was confused because there were lots of open seats. We sat down, and I laid David down in the booth to get settled in. We had been on the train about fifteen minutes—and David had dozed off—when an attendant came by and said, "Ma'am can't you find no seat?" I was confused because I thought I had a good seat! He said, "Youz' in the dining room." I think he felt sorry for us because I had a sleeping baby, so he allowed us to stay there until we arrived in St. Louis.

After an eventful overnight trip, we made it safe and sound to Bloomington. Gail was there to pick us up. We spent a week in East Peoria, and it was the best week I'd had in a long time. I wasn't looking over my shoulder constantly.

After that, we went back each year. I began making friends at their church and even dated a nice guy there, but I was far from ready to be serious about anyone. After what I had been through, I didn't think I ever wanted to get married again.

Over those few years, David and I settled into our life. By living day to day, I had even saved enough money to buy a little house. Our life, as simple as it was, was a happy life. I had taken a job at a Christian school so that I was on the same schedule as David. Life wasn't chaotic, but money was so tight. Tim refused to pay child support, and honestly, I got tired of fighting him in court. It was easier to try and make it on my own than it was to deal with him.

When I say things were tight in our house, I'm not stretching the truth. I didn't want David to know how much I struggled, so I would make a game out of it. Most weeks I couldn't afford both meat and bread, so I invented a dish called "the ham and cheese roll," which was a piece of cheese rolled up in a slice of ham, then microwaved. Gourmet, right?

On the weeks I couldn't afford meat, I invented the "mayonnaise sandwich." It was a treat if we had actual meat and bread sandwiches. It's ironic, because even when David became an adult, his favorite sandwich was a mayonnaise sandwich, which, when you think of that, it is kind of sad.

There are certain times in our lives we look back on and mark as major turning points. Here was mine. David and I were at the grocery store, and I had just enough money to get a loaf of bread and a quart of milk. I hoped the tax wouldn't go over the amount of money I had in my purse. In the checkout line, David asked if he could get a Hershey bar. I didn't have enough money to buy it. Reality set in again; how was I going to raise a child if I couldn't even afford a Hershey bar?

At the time, I had a job and was living day to day, trying to rebuild. I thought I was doing okay. But it was at that moment, when I couldn't afford a Hershey bar, that I realized just how dire my situation had become. If I was going to be able to raise David, I had to better my life. It was at this moment that I had what I call a "Scarlett O'Hara moment." I went to the car and said, "As God is my witness, I am determined to make a better life for my son!" I didn't know exactly what that looked like, but at that moment, a better life consisted of having enough money to afford a Hershey bar.

Finding Your Reason

While failing three times to get a job was my rock bottom, not being able to buy a Hershey bar was the pivotal moment when I realized I had to turn things around. My motivation to keep fighting for a better life was always David. I believe if you can find a *selfless* reason to better your life, you may stick to your plan longer and be more motivated. Selfish reasons, such as money to buy yourself a new boat, is a shallow reason to better your life, and ultimately it might not be a strong enough reason to keep you going. But if your reason is to create a better life for your family or help the world in some way, you'll be more likely to keep going.

Lots of scientific studies show that helping others can help yourself. For instance, volunteering has well-being-boosting and depression-lowering benefits. And there's now neural evidence from fMRI studies which show a link between generosity and happiness in the brain. Even donating money to others—as opposed to spending it on ourselves—activates the same regions of the brain that respond to monetary rewards or sex. We are biologically wired to feel good when we do good for others, so what could be a better motivator for bettering your life?

* EXERCISE

Find Your Who

Who do you want to help and what can you start doing today to help them?

I concluded that this was my life and I lived it. If you've suffered from a recent setback—like failing an exam or losing a job—try to find the good in the situation. Don't sit in the failure or beat yourself up. A lost job could mean more time to spend with your kids, or the opportunity to start your own business or switch career paths. I failed that exam because I wasn't meant to be a nurse. And in the end, it was all for the best, because now I'm here, living my real dream.

Remember, when God closes a door, he opens a window.

"Only for Today"

Rather than overwhelming myself with lifelong commitments, I took things one day at a time. I decided to try and live my life day by day and handle what came along.

For example, let's say you want to quit drinking soda. If you imagine depriving yourself of your favorite flavor of Coca-Cola for the rest of your life, you may get overwhelmed by the idea and decide to forget about quitting altogether. But if instead you tell yourself, "Only for today, I'm going to avoid soda," suddenly it seems pretty easy. You can do anything for a day, right?

This is a popular approach in recovery programs, and it applies to nearly any goal. Pope John XXIII says the "only for today" approach can lead to a better life. Here are his ten tips for living day to day:

1. Only for today, I will seek to live the livelong day positively without wishing to solve the problems of my life all at once.

2. Only for today, I will take the greatest care of my appearance: I will dress modestly; I will not raise my voice; I will be courteous in my behavior; I will not criticize anyone; I will not claim to improve or to discipline anyone except myself.
3. Only for today, I will be happy in the certainty that I was created to be happy, not only in the other world but also in this one.
4. Only for today, I will adapt to circumstances, without requiring all circumstances to be adapted to my own wishes.
5. Only for today, I will devote ten minutes of my time to some good reading, remembering that just as food is necessary to the life of the body, so good reading is necessary to the life of the soul.
6. Only for today, I will do one good deed and not tell anyone about it.
7. Only for today, I will do at least one thing I do not like doing; and if my feelings are hurt, I will make sure that no one notices.

8. Only for today, I will make a plan for myself; I may not follow it to the letter, but I will make it. And I will be on guard against two evils: hastiness and indecision.

9. Only for today, I will firmly believe, despite appearances, that the good Providence of God cares for me as no one else who exists in this world.

10. Only for today, I will have no fears. In particular, I will not be afraid to enjoy what is beautiful and to believe in goodness. Indeed, for twelve hours I can certainly do what might cause me consternation were I to believe I had to do it all my life.

I love that last line: "Indeed, for twelve hours I can certainly do what might cause me consternation were I to believe I had to do it all my life." This sums up the day-to-day lifestyle so simply and beautifully. And if twelve hours is even too much, take it an hour at a time, or a minute at a time.

The Next Right Thing

Another wonderful technique I discovered is doing the next right thing. If you're unsure of where you're headed in life, or what your future holds, just focus on *the next right thing*. What can you do right now to better yourself and your life? Maybe it's cleaning the house. Maybe it's sending a kind text to a friend. Maybe it's choosing the salad over the cheeseburger. Focusing just on your next action can keep things simple, and help you make better decisions more regularly. When I failed those exams, the next right thing wasn't to sulk, it was to keep looking for work. I hit the road looking for a job, which I eventually found, and went to work for a new dental office that was opening in our town.

Life is a Series of Choices

I've come to realize that life is just a series of choices. We are the choices we make. Thus far, I had been living with an attitude that everything wrong in my life had happened *to* me, and I hadn't taken responsibility for the choices I'd made to land me in those positions. I was always tempted to blame those around me—or to blame God—for whatever was going wrong in my life.

But God gives us the ability to make our own choices, and those choices have consequences. I made the choice to have sex, which led to pregnancy, which led to my marriage. I had the choice to not marry Tim, but I chose to marry him anyway. While those choices brought me a lot of pain, they also brought me my son, and he was the most amazing choice I ever made.

What choices will you make today to better your life? Listen to your conscience; your intuition can prove to be a powerful tool in telling you what's right and wrong.

ω

The year of the Hershey bar, I took my yearly trip to Illinois to visit Gail and her family. I didn't know it at the time, but my entire life was about to change. While I was visiting, Brad and Gail invited several friends over for dinner and a movie night. One of the couples there was Brad Hayes and his girlfriend, Amy. We, as usual, had an amazing time. Then at church on Sunday, Brad Hayes came up to me and explained that he owned a business and thought I would be perfect in sales. I laughed and said, "I know nothing about sales!"

He told me he was a sales trainer, and that if I moved to Illinois, he would put me to work in his company. I was stunned. I really didn't give it a lot of thought because honestly, I thought he was just being kind.

About a week after I returned home, Brad called and asked if I had given his offer any thought. I told him no, because I had thought he was just being kind. He assured me he wasn't just being kind, and he said he wanted to send some material for me to read. After studying the material, if I was interested, he was going to be in Tennessee in a few weeks and could meet with me to answer any questions I had. I thought about it and decided it wouldn't hurt to at least talk to him.

My sister Gail was encouraging me to make this move. As she reminded me, "This is the chance you've been looking for!"

After a lot of prayer and thought, I decided to give it a try. When would I ever get this kind of chance again? After all, if I went and fell on my face, I could always come back home. I talked to David and asked him if he wanted to go on an adventure. The plan was to move in with Brad and Gail until I could get established, start a new job, new school, and just have a fresh start. It was an extremely difficult and scary decision to leave everyone and everything I knew, but I decided it was the only chance I had to make a better life for David. I didn't see it then, but this opportunity was God answering a prayer and showing me how to turn things around.

We moved to East Peoria and lived with Brad, Gail, and their family. I worked for Brad Hayes until he relocated his business to Ohio, then I took another job in sales. For the first time, I thought I was actually good at something. I was making good money, we had friends at church, work, and school. Life was good.

Meanwhile, being only one of a few single people at church, everyone decided I needed to be fixed up on numerous dates. I enjoyed dating, but I *just* wanted to date. Whenever someone tried to get close, I pulled away. I decided that I would rather be by myself than to be in the type of marriage I'd been in before. I needed to find myself again, or at least a new version of myself. Obviously, the old me hadn't worked out so well.

I had an actual checklist of what I was looking for in a man. Many times, I told my friends, "If you see me walking down the aisle, I will know exactly what I'm doing." This became my motto: "I don't need a man to take care of me, I can take care of myself. I want a man who is going to love me and my son and be my best friend."

If you're in a similar circumstance where you've recently gotten out of a difficult relationship, know it's okay to just be single—for a little while, for a long while, or forever! Being single is an acceptable way of life. Before I could be part of a functional couple, I had to prove to myself that I was capable of functioning alone. Don't see being single as a punishment; it's an opportunity to find out what you *really* want from life, without someone else's desires or opinions influencing you. And once you learn to be okay by yourself, you'll be less likely to tie yourself to someone who doesn't treat you right. You'll be more confident and capable of leaving poor relationships, rather than hanging on past their due dates.

Those around you may push you to start dating sooner rather than later, but remember this is likely because they just want to see you happy, and they assume a relationship is what you want. You may also feel pressure from society, especially if you're a woman, as we are all too familiar with the "ticking clock" of our age. But resist that pressure. Being part of a couple does not equate to happiness, especially if you're in the wrong one. Remember how lonely you sometimes felt, even when you were in a relationship? Sometimes being in a bad relationship can feel much lonelier than being single.

After several years of going solo and going on more blind dates than I could possibly count, my friend and coworker Kathy told me about a friend of hers who was recently divorced and would be perfect for me. After dating so many "perfect" friends that had all ended in disaster,

I decided to decline.But on a regular basis, her friend would *miraculously* show up in places we would go. One night a group from work went to a comedy club, and Kathy introduced me to Steve, her dear friend. The entire group was loud, laughing, and having a good time. Steve sat there and hardly said a word all evening. When I tried to talk to him, all he said to me was, "You are really loud!"

Monday at work, Kathy came up to me and said, "Wow, isn't Steve wonderful?"

I responded, "I don't know, he didn't say anything all night, except for how loud I was."

Weeks went by, and Steve continued showing up. Then finally, a dozen long-stemmed, multi-colored roses showed up at my work, with a note asking me out to dinner. Honestly, I wasn't interested but since he had spent so much on the flowers, I decided to go on the date and then let him down easy.

We went to the opening night of the Peoria hockey game, had dinner, and when I got home, I realized I'd had a wonderful time. He had been very kind, and everything was so easy with him.

We had talked about a multitude of things. He asked me out again, and I decided to go, even though we knew we were total opposites.

The second date went even better than the first. There was a calmness and sincerity about him that I found intriguing. At the end of the date, he walked me to my door, gently put his hands on my face, and kissed me like I had never been kissed before. Then he just walked away. I stood at the door, speechless. And for me, that is saying something!

After our kiss, the next day I couldn't wait to call Kathy to let her know I had just kissed the man I was going to marry. He didn't quite know it yet, but it was going to happen. Her response was, "Who did you kiss?" I said, "Steve Link of course." She was floored. Just last night I had been ready to let him down easy as soon as the date was over. I let her know that she had been right all along. He was perfect for me.

Our relationship became more serious and now it was time to meet the family. When I told my mom, she was very hesitant—after all, he was a Yankee. How could you fall in love with a

Yankee? (Remember, I am a true southerner!) I brought him home at Thanksgiving and everyone was holding their breath. After all, my first choice in husbands hadn't ended well, but above all, my mother wanted me to be happy. Steve came bearing flowers for my mother, which she found to be very thoughtful. By the end of the visit, I had my mother's approval on my decision to marry Steve.

After a year of dating and getting my southern family's blessing to marry a Yankee, Steve and I were married. David walked me down the aisle, and Steve's daughter Annie was the flower girl. My brother-in-law Brad performed the ceremony, and my sister Gail was again by my side as my maid of honor. Never did I have a doubt, as I had previously told my friends, "If you see me walking down the aisle, I will know exactly what I am doing."

As David took my arm to walk me down the aisle, he said, "Mom, I will walk you down the aisle, but I'll never give you away. You will always be my mom." It was only at that moment that I began to cry.

That day, I also became the stepmother to four-year-old Anastasia, "Annie." I couldn't have known it at that moment, but this little girl would become one of the most important people in my life. She came to live full time with Steve and I when she was in fifth grade. Over the years, people would comment on how lucky she was to have me in her life, but I considered myself the lucky one. To the world, Annie was my stepdaughter, but in my heart, she was and is my daughter. She has brought so much joy into our lives. Her loving, quiet, calm spirit and her ability to think on her own is something I can only dream of. I jokingly tell her that I want to be just like her when I grow up. I may not have been there when she was born, but I have been blessed to share the past twenty-two years with her. Oh yes, I am the lucky one.

Steve and I are total opposites. He is quiet and reserved, I'm loud and outgoing. He likes tractors, I love shoes. But somehow it all works. Twenty-two years later, if he wants to get my attention, he puts his hands on my face and kisses me exactly the way he did that night. And it still leaves me speechless. Because I made a choice to not just find a husband, but to find the right husband, I now have a man who loves me unconditionally. I have a husband who, during a prayer in church, always holds my hand. I have a husband who is so thoughtful that when we have a deep snow, he backs my car into the garage so I can pull straight out of the driveway. I have a husband who no matter what hair-brained idea I have, is there to support me. My weight may go up and down, but he sees me as beautiful—always. He is truly a blessing from God.

My one wish for you is to find happiness and thrive with *whatever* relationship status you find yourself in. Make peace with wherever you are and learn to make the most of your circumstances. If you're single, relish in your freedom to do whatever you want, whenever you want. Five years from now, you may be married and watching television every evening, wishing you had enjoyed singlehood more while you had it! And if you're in the throes of casual dating, enjoy the learning experience and getting to know so many new people. And of course, if you're in love, be sure to look for the best in your partner and cherish your time with them and your family. You never know what tomorrow may bring or take.

CHAPTER 5

Five years after Steve and I married, we became concerned about David. He was twenty-two years old and working and living on his own. He'd become distant and was losing a lot of weight.

One day while I was Christmas shopping at the mall, I got a call from one of David's friends. He began the conversation by saying, "I probably shouldn't be calling you, but"—again, when a sentence starts that way, it's not going to be good—"David is taking drugs, and we think he has started using heroine."

You could have knocked me over with a feather. One minute I'm in the mall, having a great time shopping, and in an instant, one phone call turned my life upside down. I literally ran out of the mall, got in my car, and started trying to get David on the phone. I went to his house to confront him; I needed to hear it from him. Maybe his friend was making this up to get back at him for something. If this were true, why hadn't I seen it?

David admitted it was true, and I was floored. He told me he needed help but hadn't known how to tell me because he couldn't bear to see the disappointment in my face. How ironic, that was the very statement I had made to my mother when telling her I was pregnant. All I could say was, "Why would you do this to yourself?"

I was now facing the one thing I had worked all his life to keep him away from. I had always preached to him about drugs. Steve and I admitted him to rehab in Peoria, which wasn't easy. If you're under 18 years old, there are a lot of resources for getting help, but once you're an adult, it's not that easy.

After a few weeks, he was released from rehab. I was so uneducated about the subject that

I thought that once he was fixed, he was fixed for good. I was wrong. David relapsed, and Steve and I were at a loss as to what to do. We finally got David to agree to go to Tennessee, to put him in another program with the tough-love stipulation that if he didn't stay in treatment, he would no longer be welcome in our home.

If you have ever had to say that to your child, you know how heartbreaking it is. I couldn't believe God was giving me yet another cross to bear. I was so angry. I spoke to God and said, "God, why do you keep doing this to me? You can do anything to me but please don't do this to my son. Please let him realize what he is doing to himself and want to get better." I prayed for strength for myself and David.

Once again, David was released from rehab. Over the next year, he continued counseling, tried to make peace with his father, and applied to college. Little by little, he was making so much progress. He struggled with his demons but was learning to handle life in other ways, without drugs.

Drugs are a huge reality in our society. We no longer have to just worry about alcohol and marijuana; kids today are opting for prescription drugs and heroine. The kids doing these drugs are no longer just the kids from "bad" homes and poor neighborhoods; they're the kids that come from nice homes, nice families. They are not bad kids; they're just making bad choices.

The epidemic is getting worse as the years go by, and it'll continue to get worse if we don't do something. According to the CDC, in 2017 the number of overdose deaths involving opioids (including prescription opioids and illegal opioids like heroine) was six times higher than in 1999. On average, 130 Americans die every day from an opioid overdose. (REF https://www.cdc.gov/drugoverdose/epidemic/index.html). This epidemic isn't something to take lightly.

Life was becoming more normal, when without warning, David had a seizure. He was rushed to the hospital and placed under observation. After testing, the doctor seemed to think the seizure had been a fluke and that it would never happen again. While David was in rehab, he had been given a medication to lessen the side effects of withdrawal. One of the side effects was seizures. It was rare, but we were told it did happen.

A few weeks later, he had another seizure. He was consistently having seizures, and the doctor could find no reason, and no medication could get them under control. This was a constant battle, but we kept going to neurologists until finally they told us about an experimental surgery; Due to his age and otherwise good health, David was a perfect candidate. We had an appointment and I prayed harder than I had prayed for anything that God would allow this to work and David could get his life back. He had worked so hard to get clean, fight his demons, and was finally moving forward with his life.

During this time, another curveball was thrown at us; my mother was diagnosed with colon cancer. She fought for years but finally, on our wedding anniversary, November 22nd, my Mom passed away.

The following year at Christmas, David and my sister Karen came to Illinois for a visit.

Leading up to their visit, I was so excited and kept saying that it was going to be the best Christmas ever. My house was decorated like a winter wonderland, and I wanted everything to be perfect. We shopped, ate, talked, laughed, and had an amazing time.

I thought it would be a great idea to have a family picture made while we were all together. The only time the photographer could photograph us was on Christmas Eve morning. Let me tell you, getting dressed for pictures was *not* what my family wanted to do. They complained, but got dressed, went to the photography studio, and we had a blast. The photographer was such a good sport. We got finished and went home for Christmas Eve supper.

On Christmas morning, we got up to open presents, and David had a seizure while walking down the stairs and fell to the ground. We had a series of questions that we would ask him; if he could answer the questions, we weren't supposed to take him to the hospital, unless he was injured. It's very scary to see someone—especially someone you love—have a seizure. I called the neurology clinic in Nashville to see if they could get him in early and move up the surgery, but due to the holidays, they didn't have any open appointments. They assured me his appointment was only a couple weeks away, and that he should be fine.

Christmas came and went, I drove David back to Tennessee, and we spent New Year's Eve with my sister Karen watching *The Twilight Zone* marathon. This was a tradition of ours. We toasted in the New Year with Welch's grape juice, and the next day I had to return home to go back to work. I had plans to come back to Tennessee and take him to the clinic for his appointment in just a week and a half.

On January 10th, just nine days after I had returned home, Steve and I went out for dinner, and when we got home, there was a message on our phone. The voice on the other end told me my son was dead. He'd had a seizure while showering and had fallen and hit his head on the bathtub. And just like that, he was gone. I fell to my knees, and the next few weeks are pretty much a blur.

Steve and I went to Tennessee the next morning, and all I kept saying was, "I can't do this, I cannot bury my only son." With my husband and my family by my side, my brother-in-law Brad conducted my son's funeral service. I was beyond devastated. At every point of the process—from picking out the casket, picking out his clothes, writing the obituary—I would tell Steve, "I can't do this." My husband was by my side the entire time and helped me get through the service.

I had gone through many struggles in my life and had come through them with the attitude that those times had happened, that I'd survived them, and that I was a stronger person for having gone through them. But until you have looked down into a casket and seen your only child—the love of your life—nothing could have prepared me for that.

After the funeral, I cried for days. I couldn't eat, I couldn't sleep. My body would shake because I couldn't control my emotions. I had been through a lot in my life, but I had always been able to pick myself up and keep going because I had wanted a better life for my son. Everything—every decision in my life—had been for David. He was my life, my inspiration, my best friend . . . and now he was gone.

I had always identified myself as David's mother. I was no longer a mother; I had lost everything, even my identity. This time, I realized I couldn't bounce back. God had given me a blow that had totally knocked me down. I asked God again, "Why? Why did you have to take my son? Why do you keep doing this to me?" I had prayed harder than I had ever prayed in my life that my son would get better, and he died. "You are God, you can do anything. You could have stopped this."

The faith that had gotten me through everything in my life had just been pulled out from under me. The religion I had based my life on, and all the answers I had given others in this situation, no longer made sense. My 26-year-old son had been taken from this life, and nothing made sense. I stayed secluded for several weeks; I didn't even want to speak to anyone on the phone.

One day, Steve told me our minister and one of the elders wanted to come visit. I really didn't want to see them, but I agreed. My minister told me that if I wanted to talk, his door was always open. All I remember was my response, "I am way more screwed up than you are licensed for."

People gave me books, but I didn't want to read. People would bring food, but I didn't want to eat. I received a lot of cards, and for some reason, that *was* comforting for me. Each day when the mail would arrive, there would be a stack of cards. I would read and cry. I would pray and cry, "Please God, take away this pain." But the pain didn't go away. The end of the day would arrive, and I would realize I was exhausted; all I had done all day was cry. People kept telling me to take it one day at a time, but a day was too overwhelming. I was trying to get through one minute, one second at a time.

My manager—who had always been my dear friend—called one day to check on me and let me know our health insurance covered counseling. If I was interested, he would arrange the appointment for me. I had never gone to counseling but thought maybe it would take the pain away, so I agreed. I requested a female Christian counselor. For some reason, I thought a woman might better understand what I was going through.

The first day, I had no idea what to expect. My counselor asked me what had brought me to her and how could she help me. I began talking and crying. Through the tears, I told her I thought I was going crazy, that I had lost control of everything in my life. At that moment, she handed me a book and calmly asked me to read a specific page in the book out loud. The words in the book were almost word for word (minus the blubbering and crying) what I had just described to her. The book was about grief. She looked me in the eye and said, "See, my dear, you aren't going crazy, it's called grief. And I am going to help you through it."

Maybe it was the calmness in her voice, but I believed her. What a huge relief to know I wasn't going crazy. She helped me put a label on what I was feeling. She didn't take my pain away, but she taught me how to handle it. The way I describe my counseling experience was that she helped guide me through a journey that I didn't know how to navigate on my own. Through the sessions, I expressed the struggles I was having with my faith, and that I felt as if God had left me. She suggested speaking to my minister, and I did. We had several sessions, and I read a lot of books and journaled. Whatever she asked me to do, I did it.

I felt as if I was on a spiritual journey. Things I had never questioned before, I was now questioning. Things I had always believed, I was now wavering on. I was having a true crisis in my faith. When people asked me to pray for them, I would think to myself, *I don't think you want me to pray for you. Obviously, I either don't know what I'm doing, or God isn't listening to me.* I would get upset in church when "prayers were answered" for certain individuals. Why hadn't God answered my prayers, why had he let my son die? All I had asked for was a medicine or procedure that would make his seizures go away—he was God, he could do anything, right?

At one point in this journey, someone would make the comment every day, "Oh Lorie, I wish I had your strength," or, "You are so strong." I was really confused by these comments, so I mentioned them to Linda in one of our sessions. I asked her, "How can people say that? I feel so fragile that if someone blew on me, I'd crumble."

What Linda told me next was a huge breakthrough in my spiritual journey. She looked at me and said, "I know you feel like God has left you, but when people comment about your strength, it's not your strength they're seeing—it's God's. You may not be able to see it, but they can. So, every time someone mentions your strength, let that be a reminder that God has not left you. He is with you all the time."

Wow. Why couldn't I have seen that? As I began to look back, all the times I had asked for God's help, I had been expecting God to just magically take the pain away. That's not how it works, but God does offer a means to help you through your crisis.

A gospel preacher once made a comment that if we pray for bread, a loaf of Wonder Bread isn't going to come floating down from the sky, but God *can* provide a job so that we can go out and earn the money to buy the loaf of bread. When we pray to God for him to help us, that help may come in the form of a mailbox full of cards, a friend offering to help, counseling being offered, or family taking us in when we need help. God provides comfort in many ways; we need to not only ask for help but ask God to open our eyes so that when he sends help in its many forms, we take it. Throughout my life, when I had asked God for help, he was sending it. I just hadn't been able to see it.

When I asked to not be pregnant, God knew what was best and gave me the best thing that ever happened to me. God provided friends and family to be there every time I fell, to lift me up and help me go on. When I couldn't bear to tell my family that Tim was in jail, my sister Judy was there to help me through. My mother took me in when I needed a home. My sister Karen paid my bills and fed me when I most needed help. I believe God made the path for me to move to

Illinois, provided the job I have, and introduced me to my husband. I could go on and on!

At David's funeral, just when I thought I couldn't take another step, someone was there for me to lean on. That didn't just happen by accident; that was the means that God provided in answer to a prayer.

Prior to counseling, my life consisted of lying in bed and crying. Some days I brushed my hair, some days not so much. During my counseling experience, Linda pushed me to find a reason to push forward with my life. She helped me see that since David had always been my driving force to succeed, that I should try to focus on something that would help his legacy live on. As I thought on that for several weeks, I came to the realization that even though David wasn't here, I was, and I would always be his mother. If he could see me and see how sad I am, he would be very angry with me that I was lying in bed, wasting my life. He would want me to do something meaningful. That day, I made a promise to David that every single day, no matter how difficult it was, I would get up and do something to make him proud. Some days, that was sending a card to someone who needed encouragement. Some days, it was just getting up and brushing my hair. But either way, I wasn't lying in bed crying. Was it easy? No, but I still try every day to keep that promise.

If you were to pass away tomorrow, wouldn't you want your loved ones to continue living life to its fullest? You wouldn't want them to waste their precious time on earth; you would want them to get out there and make an impact. If you've recently lost someone you love, how would they want you to spend the rest of your time here on Earth? It likely doesn't include feeling sorry for yourself or lying around. Honor them by living your life the way they would've wanted you to.

Along my journey, I did a lot of soul searching, meditating, study of scripture, and talking to my minister, friends, family, or anyone that would listen! I came to realize that God hadn't left me, he had been there the whole time. I had just refused to acknowledge it. The phrase "hindsight is 20/20" is so true. We can't always see what's right in front of us. It wasn't until years later that I could look back on my life and see everything and everybody God had put in my path along the way. As they're happening, we call them coincidences, but I no longer believe in coincidences—everything happens for a reason.

* EXERCISE

Where is God?

God hasn't left you. Starting today, look for Him in ways you wouldn't expect—in a stranger's smile, a blue sky, or an unexpected opportunity. By exercising this habit daily, you'll gain a new superpower: the ability to see and feel God in every moment.

CHAPTER 6

Growing up, David was a loud, outgoing, and energetic boy. Baseball was his passion. He began playing little league and continued playing through middle school. From grades 6-8, he had a paper route that allowed him to purchase his favorite collectable: baseball cards. On Fridays, he would collect his pay, then Saturday afternoon he'd go to the local baseball card store to buy, sell, or trade with the owner. I wasn't comfortable with him walking his paper route alone that early in the morning, so I would drive the route with him, then we would go to Hardee's and eat breakfast. We solved all the world's problems over many sausage and biscuit sandwiches.

I'm not sure where he got it from, but he was talented in drawing and art. He would sit for hours drawing until he got the picture exactly right. His other passion was WWE wrestling. He and his best friend, James, would play wrestling for hours. They even created their own virtual wrestling world, complete with all the artwork by David. They created virtual characters who would wrestle each other. They collected all the action figures and spent many hours bonding over the sport.

David's sense of humor was contagious. He was a practical joker, and no one could make me laugh the way he did. It was a tradition that on April Fools' Day, we would try to outdo the other with a prank. Most of the time, he was the winner. Holidays were very special with us, and we celebrated to the fullest.

Being a mother was my greatest joy, but being a single mother was extremely difficult. Every decision had to be made by me and only me. Every bill needed to be paid by me and only me. Small decisions such as what to have for supper had to be made by me. At times, I wished for someone to just help me make all the decisions that needed to be made in a day. How would I afford Christmas presents, braces, or any emergency that would arise? There were times when he was growing so fast, I would buy jeans in January, and by April he would have outgrown them. And feeding a growing boy . . . wow he could eat!

I tried not to let him know how difficult life was for us, so I always tried to make life an adventure for him. At Christmas, when money was tight, I would set up a scavenger hunt for him to find his presents. We would wake up early on Christmas, have a special breakfast, and then head to the tree. There would be a poem wrapped up under the tree with clues in the lyrics. He would follow the clues to find his presents. In our home, Santa still comes to visit. Not the man in the red suit, but the magic of what it feels like to anticipate the surprise.

The bond we had was strong, so strong that sometimes even Steve didn't understand it. Maybe because of all the years we had struggled together, at times it had seemed like it was us against the world. We talked about everything, prayed together, shared our secrets, played together, and because I was only eighteen when he was born, sometimes I felt like we had grown up together. I was his mother, but also his friend. When he would call me, I could immediately tell what type of mood he was in just by the sound of his voice. I loved him with every ounce of my being.

I don't just miss David; I miss so many things about him. After he died, I found no joy in day-to-day activities. I didn't want to laugh or have a good time. That made me feel as though I was in some way dishonoring his memory. How could I ever laugh again? How could I laugh and have a good time, when my world was now gone? Simple tasks became a hardship. Even after he was grown, I would buy his favorite things and make a "care package" to send to him. He loved receiving those in the mail. We also had fun picking out Hallmark cards to send to one another.

After he died, I ventured out on my first trip to the grocery store, telling myself that I could do this. It took me days to build myself up for that trip. I grabbed a cart and began throwing items in, trying to get in and out as fast as I could, before seeing anyone I knew. It was going well, until I got to the potato chip aisle. David's favorite chips were the Lay's cheddar and sour cream, which I had always purchased to go in his care packages. Knowing I could no longer buy those chips caused me to have a small breakdown in the snack aisle. Yes . . . the snack aisle. I left my filled cart and ran to the car as fast as I could.

When you lose someone, of course you mourn for all the big moments in life you will never have. I knew I would never see him get married or have children. I didn't get to see him finish college. No more birthdays or Christmas scavenger hunts. But what I miss most are the little things: those day-to-day things like buying his favorite potato chip, hearing his voice on the other end of the phone, calling me to tell me his joke of the day, and hardest of all is never being called "Mom" again.

It took me a long time—and a lot of lessons learned—to start living life after David's passing. But once I started living life again, the results were beautiful. I became a vibrant, strong woman again, and my sister Gail told me how proud of me she was. "You should write a book," she said. "Your life is more interesting than a lot of Lifetime movies." (I have seen a lot of Lifetime movies, and they typically don't end well.)

I didn't know how to write a book, so I decided one day to just start writing some of my stories down. I made a journal of all that had happened to me along my journey, and how far I had come. Not only was the journaling cathartic, but it helped me to see all my progress. It was empowering to see how much I'd overcome; how much I had grown.

✻ EXERCISE

Start a journal.

If you don't already journal on a daily basis, I highly recommend you do so. Journaling increases mindfulness and helps give perspective on your life. There's something powerful about getting your thoughts on paper. A problem that seems unsolvable in your head can suddenly have a clear solution when you put it down on paper. Journaling can also increase your ability to perceive and manage your own emotions and those of others.

One day, some of my friends were headed to a Ladies Day conference in Indiana. One of my friends asked me why I didn't agree to speak for a Ladies conference. A lightbulb went off in my head. A portion of my current job—the same job I had at the time—is to speak in front of groups of people, so public speaking isn't and wasn't a fear of mine. I didn't know how to write a book, but I definitely knew how to talk! Speaking professionally seemed like a perfect path for me.

I came home that weekend and spent months putting together "my story," as though I was presenting it in front of a group. But to be honest, I didn't really know what I was going to do with it! When I finished, I sent it to my sister Gail for her to read and critique. After a few days, she called me crying. I asked her what was wrong, and she told me that she had read my story and that it had touched her so much. I thought this reaction was odd, since she had lived most of it alongside me. She said she hadn't seen it all from my perspective. She encouraged me to go forward with it, to share it with others.

After speaking at my local congregation in 2016, I was invited by a church in Michigan to speak for a fee. I stepped back because it was never part of the plan to take money. My purpose has always been to help struggling women by showing them how they can get through those difficult times. I knew I needed to be more polished in my speaking before feeling "good enough" to take a fee, but I wasn't sure how that would happen.

I prayed, "God, if this is what I'm supposed to do, please unlock that door and show me what I need to do." Four weeks later, in March 2018, I took a doctor to a business institute seminar sponsored by my company. It was a four-day course with about sixteen people, so we all got to know each other quite well by the end of the seminar. The first speaker to address the group was Katherine. When she introduced herself, she made the statement that several of the Henry

Schein (my company) people may know her because she coaches executives to speak in a public forum. I was intrigued, so I sat by her that night at dinner. As the evening went on, I thought we had gotten to know each other well enough that I could ask her a question: "I know you said you train executives to speak for groups, but if just some random person wants to polish her skills, is that something you do?"

She asked me to explain a little bit about what I meant, and I told her what I was doing with my speech. She happens to also be all about empowering women and has two seminars at her ranch every year. The next one was coming up in the fall, she sent me the info, and I signed up.

In November, I flew to San Diego and took her course. She was so encouraging of what I was doing. Everyone at the seminar was there for business-related speaking, so I was the only one there for personal reasons. She had mentioned I should write a book or conduct a seminar for women, but again, both of those were totally foreign to me. But I kept the ideas in the back of my mind. After all, I had the feeling God had brought her to me.

After returning home, I worked on my speech using the tools I had been taught by Katherine. After thinking more about it, I decided to at least explore the possibility of taking this as far as I could. After all, I had prayed my prayer and in just four weeks, Katherine had popped into my life. Again, I asked God that if this was what he wanted me to do, to lead me where he wanted me to go. I called Katherine to see what the next step would be. She introduced me to Mark, a business and development coach, in February 2019. I sent him a copy of my story, and his response was that he was overcome with emotion after reading it. He was an amazing help and huge source of encouragement for me.

With his help, over the next few months I developed a marketing plan, set up a business, named the business, created a logo, and put together my speech in a more polished format with a title. The final piece of that puzzle was Mark introducing me to Kristen Forbes, an editor who is taking my words and putting them into a book. For those who wonder if God answers prayers, just look at this chain of events. He can turn the impossible, into possible. I don't know where this will take me, but I am so grateful to all the people along the way who have believed in me and gotten me to this point.

It isn't easy to share this story, but I stand on the stage and wrote this book because I want to help other women see that no matter what they have gone through in the past, they don't have to be defined by that story. I have a beautiful family and home. I now work for a Fortune 500 company. I do not tell you these things out of ego, but to show you that no matter what you have gone through, you can come through it if you choose to take that first step. My first step was a promise to my son. I made the choice that I would not be defined by the things that happened to me in my past, but by the things I choose to accomplish in my life today. I want to be defined by my strength, my incredible family, and my service to others.

If you aren't sure of what's next for you in your life, answer this question: What do you have to give? I have my story and the lessons I learned from an arduous life. I decided to share that story in order to help other women. We all have a gift to give and a role to play. You were brought into this life for a reason, and your number one job is to find out what that reason is. What were you brought here to do, to contribute to the world? Stop focusing on what the world is doing *to* you and start focusing on what you can do for the world.

* EXERCISE

What's your gift?

> There's no better feeling in life than sharing your gift with others. But, of course, this requires finding that gift first!

Sometimes, we confuse a *learned talent* with an inherent gift. A learned talent is something you've become good at through practice, but it isn't necessarily what you were born to do, and you likely don't fully enjoy the activity itself.

For example, a person who works at a women's clothing store for five years may become very good at selling clothing, simply out of years of daily practice, but that doesn't mean selling is the person's inherent gift. An inherent gift is likely something you enjoyed doing even as a child or teenager, something that brought you natural joy from the very first time you tried it. Think back to various times in your life when you felt giddy or got goosebumps. What were you doing?

Write a list of at least ten of these special moments in your life and look for possible triggers. For example, if you write "being captain of the high school bowling team," you may be a natural leader or enjoy inspiring and cheering on others. It doesn't necessarily mean your calling is bowling, so look for the subtext.

Once you figure out your gift, you can incorporate it into your life in any way that makes sense to you right now. Don't overwhelm or pressure yourself into making a major life change. For example, if you find out your inherent gift is teaching, you don't necessarily need to quit your day job and become a full-time high school math teacher. Maybe you start by volunteering to tutor a few hours a month or getting more involved in your own child's education by helping them with homework every night.

Once I figured out my inherent gift was my story and the lessons I've learned, I started out slowly by sharing my story at small events, free of charge. Over time, this built into more and more paid speaking engagements. And now it's developed into this book. Take things one step at a time. And remember to enjoy the ride!

As you move forward in your life, remember these lessons:

1. **We are the choices we make in this life.**

   While I believe God has a plan, he also gives us freedom of choice. Earlier in my life, I blamed God for so many things: my pregnancy, Tim's imprisonment, David's passing. But I came to realize that I had made the choices that put me on the path of my destruction. God didn't cause me to get pregnant, God didn't cause Tim to make the choices he did that put him in prison, and no one made David take those drugs. We made those choices, and we paid the consequences for our actions.

The beautiful thing about taking responsibility for your actions is that you can feel empowered to make better choices in the future. Better choices have better consequences. The mistakes you've made in your life can't be undone; you can't go back in time and change them. You must accept this fact and move forward. Focus on what you can do today, right now, to better your life.

2. **God will never leave us.**

   God is always there, even if we can't see Him. We may move away from Him, but He is always there for us. God doesn't cause bad things to happen, but He is there to help us through them. We need to keep our eyes open to see all the ways He is there: a job that will put us on a path to a better life, a family who opens their home when we need a place to live, cards in the mail when we've lost a loved one, a friend who sets up counseling appointments when we can't find our way.

God may not answer your prayers in the way you expect, but that doesn't mean He isn't there. Remind yourself every morning to keep your eyes peeled for God's presence and the gifts He is sending your way.

3. **Perfection is a myth.**

Everyone is fighting their own version of chaos. No one is perfect. Do not fear being judged or looked down upon by others. Do not suffer in silence just to keep up appearances; ask for help when you need it. By keeping your problems and negative emotions to yourself, you are giving them more power. Release that tension by sharing your struggles with a friend, relative, or licensed professional.

I wouldn't be where I am today if I had continued keeping my problems to myself. From sharing my marital problems with my sister, to being honest and open with a counselor, sharing has immensely changed my life. Humans were not meant to go through the struggles of life alone. Find a support system, and do not be afraid to lean on them in times of need.

4. **Rock bottom gives you firm ground to stand on.**

   Hitting bottom can catapult you into transformation. Life's greatest lessons can be learned during the most painful moments. Take this opportunity to grow, learn, and innovate yourself. Look for the lesson to be learned. Because of the struggles I've gone through, I've learned that I'm a much stronger person than I ever knew. I learned that I'm worthy of love. I learned to stand on my own two feet and become a successful businesswoman. I learned that I didn't need a man to take care of me, that I can take care of myself. I became a more driven person, someone who was willing to do what was necessary to give my son the life he deserved. Without all the struggles I went through, I wouldn't be where I am now.

5. **The darkness will pass.**

   Life is all about phases. If you're in a dark spot, remember the sun always comes back out. The dark times of our lives don't last forever. Eventually, you will feel joy again. I promise you will. In the meantime, reach out to others, connect with God, and do your best to be grateful for what you *do* have. You have the power to change your life, and you can start today.

☙

As I conclude this book, I want to thank you from the bottom of my heart for reading my story. I hope it has inspired or helped you in some way. I truly believe you have the ability to do and be whatever you choose.

Today, I enjoy a fulfilling life, one I share with a loving man who is also my best friend. We are total opposites—but that keeps our life interesting! He is completely supportive of this endeavor, and I totally support his craziness also. We make a great team. At the time of writing this book, we have been married for twenty-two wonderful years. You too can have a life you love living—it's yours for the taking. All you have to do is reach out and grab it.

ABOUT THE AUTHOR

Lorie Link is a Mother, wife, sister and friend with an undying spirit to help others see God even through challenges.

Through speaking and her book, Link to Hope, One woman's journey to find her way, Lorie shares her personal story, a message of courage, compassion, and friendship. Each step of life gives us choices-and every choice a consequence. Even in the darkest of times, God is there to offer help-just ask for it. Though not easy, you can survive tragedy. With God, you are stronger than you think.

Originally from a small town in Middle Tennessee, Lorie now lives in Illinois with her husband Steve. She enjoys traveling, serving her community, shoe shopping, and spending time with family and friends.

Made in the USA
Monee, IL
06 July 2021

73060103R10072